GUIDE FOR TRUTH SEEKING CHRISTIANS

GUIDE FOR
Truth-Seeking Christians

RALPH WEIMANN

Foreword by Robert Cardinal Sarah

Copyright © Ralph Weimann 2023

All rights reserved.
No part of this book may be reproduced
or transmitted, in any form or by any
means, without permission.

ISBN: 978-1-990685-84-2

Arouca Press
PO Box 55003
Bridgeport PO
Waterloo, ON N2J 0A5
Canada
www.aroucapress.com
Send inquiries to info@aroucapress.com

CONTENTS

Foreword ix

Introduction...................... xv

1 Can the Truth be Known and Professed? . . . 1

2 Faith: Is it More than a Pious Fairy Tale? . . . 5

3 Can Everyone be Blessed According
   to his Own Fancy? 8

4 Does it Matter Which Religion
   You Choose?..................... 11

5 Do Christians Have to be
   Like Everyone Else?.............. 15

6 Are all People Children of God:
   Why is Baptism Needed?.......... 19

7 Religion Yes, Church No? 23

8 Is the Catholic Church in Possession
   of the Truth? 27

9 May the Church Prescribe
   a Moral Code? 31

10 The Pope: Infallible?............... 35

11 Is the Church too Fixated on the
   Sacraments?..................... 39

12 Is There a Difference Between Priests
   and Lay People? 43

13 Is Confession Outdated? 47

14 Is the Eucharist More than
   a Meal for All? 50

15 Can Sundays and Solemnities
   be Cancelled?. 54

16 Is Mary a Role Model for Self-Determination
   and Women's Rights?. 58

17 Angels and Saints:
   More than an Edifying Tale? 62

18 Heaven for all – or,
   What Comes After Death? 66

   Afterword. 71

FOREWORD

I AM PLEASED TO WRITE THE FOREword to the book *Guide for Truth Seeking Christians*. The author is a German priest, Father Ralph Weimann, who holds a doctorate in theology and bioethics and is a professor at the Pontifical University of St. Thomas Aquinas (Angelicum) in Rome. He is also a member of the "New Circle of Disciples of Joseph Ratzinger."

For more than fifty years, there has been an ongoing dispute about the interpretation of the Second Vatican Council, with many referring to a supposed "spirit of the Council." The foundations of the faith are even being called into question and consequently the Church today is in crisis, which is evident in the progressive erosion of its dogmatic and moral teaching. It is no secret that many Christians in our time are seeking the truth, however they are disoriented and often completely confused.

In his 2005 address to the Roman Curia, Benedict XVI noted that "even without wishing to apply to what occurred in these years the description that St Basil, the great Doctor of the Church, made of the Church's situation after the Council of Nicea," there are similarities. Basil "compares her situation to a naval battle in the darkness of the storm, saying among other things: 'The raucous shouting of those who through disagreement rise up against one another, the incomprehensible chatter, the confused din of uninterrupted clamoring, has now filled almost the whole of the Church, falsifying through excess or failure the right doctrine of the faith...'" (Benedict XVI, Address to the Roman Curia, 22 December 2005).

It is no wonder that many Christians today are confused. Even the content of the creed is frequently put up for discussion and the faithful Christian is exposed to a variety of contradictory opinions. There are those within the Church who feel transported back to the 4th century, when Basil the Great (†379) addressed the bishops of Italy and Gaul and complained bitterly that those who persecute and question the faith are calling themselves "Christians." He wrote: "The scrupulous observance of the traditions of the Fathers is now terribly punished as a crime. The God-fearing are cast out of their homes and banished to the wastelands." Believers today who want to hold on to the faith of their forefathers are subject to a similarly painful experience. They face the loss

Foreword

of their spiritual home, they are ridiculed and labeled as backward-looking, they are opposed and scattered, and often they are even told that there is no place for them in the Church.

This challenge ignores a fundamental fact: there can be no progress in faith without fidelity to the faith of our forefathers. St. Paul therefore recommends to Timothy to fight the good fight of faith: "for I remember your sincere faith, which was already alive in your grandmother Loïs and in your mother Eunice, and which now, I know, lives also in you" (2 Tim. 1:5). Pope Benedict XVI wrote: "What was sacred to previous generations remains sacred and great to us as well; it cannot suddenly be forbidden all around or even harmful." This is not a matter of holding on to the old for the sake of the "good old days," but of being faithful to the source, which is Jesus Christ. He is the newness that can never be surpassed at any time. Therefore, it is necessary to hold on to Him.

More urgently than ever, believers need doctrinal and moral teaching, as well as reliable orientation and guidance. They must not be left to sort through conflicting opinions, or they risk going astray. Teaching the ignorant and counseling the doubtful are among the spiritual works of mercy. This service to the truth, which is Jesus

Christ himself (cf. John 14:6), is of fundamental importance in our times. It is to the credit of Father Ralph Weimann, a theologian who is particularly attentive to the current challenges of the Church, but at the same time deeply rooted in the great tradition of the Church, to have made a valuable contribution to answering these challenges in the present book, *Guide for Truth Seeking Christians.*

The book examines 18 topics related to the articles of the Creed, which are the basis of our faith. Thus, it becomes clear that faith is reasonable and through it the invisible God becomes visible, and that he has irrevocably revealed himself in Jesus Christ. The Church's role is to be the instrument of salvation and to bring the presence of God into the world, especially through the sacraments. A look at the sacramental structure of the Church demonstrates that the believer is not alone but is in communion with God, the angels and the saints. Human life receives its meaning and value from God.

This book offers guidance that leads Christians to Jesus Christ, the Son of the living God. To this end, each chapter first addresses common prejudices leveled against the faith and the Church. Then, based on Holy Scripture and Tradition, an answer is given to each of these challenges. This book is a valuable help especially for confused believers but also useful for every Catholic who wants to be ready to "speak and answer" about his faith (1 Pet. 3:15).

It is therefore my desire that this book be widely distributed so that believers may become authentic witnesses to the Gospel, preserving and living it in order to remain in communion with the living God and worship Christ as their King and Lord.

On the Solemnity of Our Lord Jesus Christ
King of the world, November 26, 2023
✠Robert Card. Sarah

INTRODUCTION

MORE THAN 40 YEARS AGO, HANS URS von Balthasar published a book called "Short Primer for Unsettled Laymen." In the preface, he lays out his concern which will also be our focus, namely that theologians are often responsible for the confusion of Christians who simply believe in Jesus Christ and want to follow his message. Von Balthasar compares those theologians with the scribes and Pharisees, whom the Lord calls "hypocrites" because they close the way to the kingdom of heaven for people and do not enter it themselves (cf. Matt. 23:12).

Since then, this tendency has only intensified. The unequivocal fidelity to revealed truth is equated with fundamentalism, while the questioning of even the most basic truths of faith is tolerated and encouraged. The admonition in the first letter of John takes on new meaning in this context: "They came from among us, but they did not belong to us" (1 John 2:19). Belonging to Jesus Christ, who revealed Himself as the way, the truth and the life (cf. John 14:6), presupposes recognizing and following *His* truth.

Today, there is a contrary tendency. For many, the standard for belief is no longer the truth revealed in Jesus Christ, but whatever matches their own desires and preferences. By living according to personal preferences, they measure themselves against ever-changing societal standards. Moreover, by applying complicated "scientific" methods that are often difficult for the layman to understand, "modern" theologians embrace new standards for faith. They claim that times have changed and that in today's world faith must be determined by other paradigms. Criticism or objections to this new standard for faith are increasingly ignored.

But faith is based neither on majorities nor on the ever-changing zeitgeist, nor is it the mouthpiece of the cultural mainstream, but rather it is a personal response to God, who reveals himself. "But faith is the foundation of things hoped for, a coming to light of facts not seen" (Heb. 11:1). Accordingly, faith is preceded by the revelation of God. Against this background, the apostle's admonition, which is always valid, becomes understandable: "There are some who are disturbing you and wish to pervert the gospel of Christ. But even if we or an angel from heaven should preach to you a gospel other than the one that we preached to you, let that one be accursed!" (Gal. 1:7–8).

Introduction

The Gospel, as a guideline for one's life, can only unfold its power if it is accepted in faith. Doubt, which unsettles many people today, is contrary to faith (cf. James 1:6), because whoever doubts in faith ultimately doubts Jesus Christ. The Church therefore speaks of a "light of faith," whereby God and the way to Him become visible. This light of faith threatens to go out in many and a kind of "vicious circle" develops: Through a purposeful questioning of the revealed truth, the faithful are unsettled. Just as the constant drop erodes the stone, the constant doubt erodes the faith. As a result, the profession of faith as an expression of faith becomes invalid, because a profession without conviction is worthless. This leads to the loss of credibility.

This vicious circle can only be broken if at the beginning there is no doubt, which is incidentally *the* temptation of the devil par excellence (cf. Gen. 3:1), but rather if there is the immovable "foundation of what is hoped for". Then and only then is there an answer to the request: "He who seeks finds; and to him who knocks, the door will be opened" (Matt. 7:8).

This booklet aims to provide guidance in this regard. It wants to help Christians seeking truth to find clarity in order to live the faith despite increasing headwinds. Based on God's revelation, transmitted through Scripture and Tradition by the Church, the following explanations offer answers to some of the most common questionings of the faith. The first step is to present each issue before providing a response.

1

Can the Truth be Known and Professed?

SPEAKING ABOUT "TRUTH" frightens many because they associate those who claim to speak truth with narrow-mindedness and intolerance. This tendency is even more pronounced regarding "apologetics," which has fallen into disrepute as the "defense" of the faith for several reasons. Defending the faith seems disreputable to many, because whoever defends himself is under accusation and seems to have something to hide. Secondly—it is claimed—the categories of "true" and "false" can no longer be used today. Due to the progress of science and the complexity of the modern world, in the opinion of many, a clear positioning is simply not possible. At best, an approximation to the truth is possible. If this view were correct, it would have severe consequences for revealed truth. If truth cannot be established, how would a profession of the truth be possible?

In answering this question, a fundamental misunderstanding must first be cleared up. While apologetics derives from the Greek language, where it was understood to be defensive writing, apologetics has taken on a new and broader meaning in Christianity. The First Letter of Peter says, "Always be ready to give an answer [*apologia*] to anyone who asks about the reasonableness [*logos*] of the hope that fills you" (1 Pet. 3:15). Apologetics, then, is much more than a defense of the faith; it is about showing the reasonableness and inner logic of the faith.

Apologetics is rooted in the basic assumption that faith is not irrational, but rather super-rational, in that it shows a perspective that does not end in the here and now but leads to eternal life. Faith is the human response to divine revelation (*logos*), which as *the* truth provides the basic structure of Christianity. Christian faith is not based on ideas or theories developed by human beings, but on God, who revealed himself in Jesus Christ as "the way and the truth and the life" (John 14:6). Whoever rejects this truth rejects the Christian faith because he rejects Jesus Christ.

Can the Truth be Known and Professed?

While we cannot possess the truth, we can participate in it and consequently we are able to recognize it. It would be the opposite of humility to deny faith the claim to truth, it would ultimately be the negation of God. Because God communicated Himself in a new way through His incarnation, true humility consists in not subjecting this divine reality to one's own standards, but conversely to subordinate oneself to the divine standard. In the beginning was the divine Word (cf. John 1:1), the reasonableness inscribed in faith.

This basic structure of Christianity has made possible the emergence of universities whose foundations are of ecclesiastical origin (such as the *Sorbonne* in Paris, *La Sapienza* in Rome, the *University of Oxford*, etc.), even if this is often suppressed today, especially since the Church is falsely portrayed as hostile to science. Already Justin the Martyr (†165) was aware that it is the task of every Christian to "speak and answer" to everyone who asks about Jesus Christ. However, this can only succeed if the faith is true and the believer accepts this truth in life, seeks to penetrate it in order to finally be able to pass it on.

In recent decades, a process of secularization has taken place that is becoming more and more radical and is leading to religious illiteracy. Therefore, it is imperative to show the inner reasonableness and beauty of faith. The profession of Jesus Christ as Lord and Savior is a profession of truth, which is recognizable and liberating (cf. John 8:32).

2

Faith: Is it More than a Pious Fairy Tale?

PUBLIC PERCEPTION OF THE Catholic faith is often that it is a pious fairy tale or a type of consolation for those needing hope of an afterlife. The enlightened person, it is argued, no longer needs such fairy tales. The Protestant theologian and New Testament scholar Rudolf Karl Bultmann (†1976) summed up this attitude when he stated in 1941: "One cannot use electric light and radio... and at the same time believe in the spirit and miracle world of the New Testament" (Rudolf Bultmann, *Neues Testament und Mythologie*, 73). Is faith just a pious fairy tale? What is it about?

To answer these questions, some fundamental explanations must first be given. With a rationalistic (reason alone) and immanentist (limited to the here and now) thinking there is indeed no place for faith. The basic problem consists in a methodological narrowness. As important as visible and thus provable facts are, they can only capture a fraction of reality. Love, spiritual abilities, and thus also the question of God remain outside rational thought alone.

"God is spirit" (John 4:23) and thus withdrawn from positivistic science, which is limited to the visible. Faith, on the other hand, opens a broader perspective that includes the supernatural—that is, what goes beyond nature. That man is not constrained in the here and now, but is directed toward God, was already explained by St. Augustine in the profound words: "You (God) have created us for Yourself, and our heart is restless until it rests in You." In this way he expressed what is fundamental in the order of creation: man, created in the image of God (cf. Gen. 1:27), has an immortal soul. Without God, the source of immortality, the creature falls into nothingness (Vatican II, *Gaudium et Spes*, 36).

God is not at all a projection of man, but a reality which is the origin and the goal of every life. He is Creator and Finisher or, as the Scriptures say, "the beginning and the end" (Rev. 22:13). Only in God is the meaning of life revealed, only

Faith: Is it More than a Pious Fairy Tale?

in him is fulfillment to be found, which does not end with death but leads to eternal life.

God's presence is inscribed in nature, it is recognizable (cf. Rom. 1:19) and it is the foundation of true rationality. Moreover, God has revealed himself, for he entered the world and came to impart his wisdom (cf. Eph. 1:9). This was done in an unsurpassable way in the incarnation of Jesus Christ, so that we might receive a share in the divine nature (cf. 2 Pet. 1:4). The revelation of Jesus Christ (Greek also = *logos*) is the starting and reference point for faith, which is not only logical, but the only way to do justice to the inner makeup of man (i.e., the soul). Faith is therefore man's response to God revealing himself and therefore necessary for salvation. For whoever believes and is baptized will be saved (cf. Mak 16:16).

The denial of God does not lead to an increase in rationality, but rather to a loss of meaning and by extension a loss of dignity. If this is done with reference to science, then science becomes unscientific, because its method does not allow such statements. If a theologian denies the supernatural reality, he ceases to be a theologian since God (Greek = *Theós*) is beyond the category of "nature," being the uncreated Creator.

3

Can Everyone be Blessed According to his Own Fancy?

FREDERICK THE GREAT († 1786), who was a Protestant and a Freemason, said that everyone should be blessed according to his or her own fancy. One of the most influential theologians of the last century, Karl Rahner († 1984), expressed this more pointedly. He went so far as to say that someone could be a Christian anonymously, without an explicit practice of the faith as taught by the Catholic Church. Such an idea is widespread among Catholics today. Many want to believe in some way and in something, but only according to one's own ideas. They distance themselves from clear guidelines or even directives, so that in the end neither *creed* nor *dogma* nor *Magisterium*

Can Everyone be Blessed According to his Own Fancy?

is granted any binding authority. The question is therefore of importance: Can everyone be blessed according to his or her own ideas of the faith? Can faith be separated from specific practice and from the contents of Church teaching?

The essential characteristic of Christianity is faith in a personal God who has revealed himself in Jesus Christ. Therefore, the acceptance of Jesus Christ is the prerequisite for faith. Faith presupposes conversion: "Repent and believe in the gospel!" (Mark 1:15). The letter to the Ephesians describes it this way: "Put off the old man of the former way of life, which perishes in the lusts of deceit, and be renewed by the Spirit in your mind!" (Eph. 4:22–23). Conversion is *the* precondition for being a Christian and leads to a new perspective. The determining factor for the believer is the revelation of God, not one's own desires and ideas. The Acts of the Apostles testifies that the disciples became believers through conversion and were therefore called Christians (cf. Acts 11:19–26). Already in this passage it becomes clear that no one can be blessed according to his own beliefs, but only once he begins to follow Christ.

Christ did not reveal himself in arbitrariness, but as "the way and the truth and the life" (John 14:6). His incarnation means that God becomes tangible and as such provides a concrete way. Only those who take this "new path"—as Christianity was called at the beginning—become Christians (cf. Matt. 16:24). It is about a concrete life decision, because "he who has my commandments and keeps them is he who loves me" (John 14:21). A faith that would refrain from this or renounce it would be a dead faith (cf. James 2:17–24). It would be an expression of neo-paganism or New Age practice.

Revelation precedes faith and through the acceptance of revelation, which is Jesus Christ himself, man becomes a Christian. Therefore, faith and practice cannot be separated, because God did not anonymously become man. He came into the world from heaven for us men and for our salvation. This truth of faith is laid down in the solemn profession of faith (*Credo*) as a standard for one's life. Accordingly, salvation is bound to the acceptance of this truth: "As high as the heavens are above the earth, so high are my ways above your ways and my thoughts above your thoughts" (Isa. 55:9). Therefore, basic trust—that God knows better than we do—precedes faith. He knows our needs (cf. Matt. 6:8). Holding fast to the truths of faith means holding fast to Jesus Christ as He has revealed Himself. In this way, the promise of sharing in eternal life is fulfilled (cf. 1 John 2:25).

4

Does it Matter Which Religion You Choose?

IN TIMES OF INTERRELIGIOUS dialogue and intercultural coexistence, the impression is often given that all religions are somehow equal. What religions have in common is that they give expression to an inner search of man, and this is put forth as the most important element of religion. Another much-touted commonality of multiple religions is that they reflect in a different way a belief in the one God. Frequently, a Hindu parable is cited to support this thesis. According to this parable, a king in northern India invited all blind people to touch an elephant. Each of them touched a different part of the elephant, which led to different opinions about the elephant's appearance, and in the end to a heated argument, which the king enjoyed. This is how the coexistence of the different religions is understood today and consequently seems to make no difference whether someone ends up being a Catholic, a Protestant, a Muslim, a Buddhist or a member of any other religion. So, does it make a difference which religion one chooses? To better answer this question, we will first look at the origin of the Christian religion.

The Christian believes in Jesus Christ as the Son of God. He was born of the Father before all time; he became man and entered into human history and was born of the Virgin Mary. God revealed Himself to show us a path that does not end with death, but leads to eternal life, which only God is able to give. This revelation marks a turning point in the history of humanity. God is not an unrecognizable, abstract entity, but he has revealed himself with a face and a name, through which he has become recognizable. Even more, Jesus Christ reveals himself as *the* truth (cf. John 14:6). The acceptance of this truth is the way that leads to salvation, and this happens in faith, which is consequently necessary for salvation (cf. Mark 16:16). It comes alive in love.

Through the revelation of Jesus as the Son of God, man is no longer blindly grasping for the unknown; rather, "he who seeks finds" (Matt. 7:8). He who seeks does not find emptiness, but God, who has revealed Himself so that He can be found. From this logic, it becomes understandable why the second Epistle of John calls the one who does not confess Jesus as Christ—as the Son of God—antichrists (cf. 2 John 7). For the incarnation of Jesus Christ leads to a separation of spirits, either one enters his discipleship to have eternal life, or one rejects salvation (cf. Luke 9:23–26). This becomes even clearer against the background of redemption. Jesus Christ dies on the cross, as the mediator of divine grace. It is here, in the moment of unconditional surrender, that he opens the gate to eternal life for all who believe in him. This mediation of salvation, which in its uniqueness is comparable to nothing that has ever been or will ever be, is conditional upon the believer's acceptance of Jesus' necessary role in our salvation: for "there is no other name under heaven given among men by which we must be saved" (Acts 4:12).

This makes it clear why the Lord calls himself *the* door: "whoever enters through me will be saved" (John 10:9). Conversely, this means that there can be no more new public revelation (cf. Vatican II, *Dei Verbum*, 4) before the glorious return of Christ. Because God has revealed Himself once and for all in the incarnation of Jesus Christ, there is no other way to salvation except through Him. Dialogue with other religions is always possible for a Christian when it becomes a *dia-logos*, that is an encounter with the truth that has revealed itself in its fullness in Jesus Christ.

5

Do Christians Have to be Like Everyone Else?

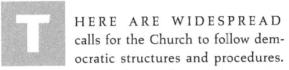HERE ARE WIDESPREAD calls for the Church to follow democratic structures and procedures. This extends to calls for equality even in appointments to offices within the Church. There is a push for the church to "dare" to be more democratic and use "creative" and "courageous" changes in order to achieve this goal in the Church. These demands are voiced through petitions, academic writings, the organization of discussion forums, etc. There is no lack of ingenuity in the pressure mechanisms used to bring about increased democracy within the Church. Media and societal support for these demands for institutional change are assured because the demands conform

GUIDE FOR TRUTH-SEEKING CHRISTIANS

to current societal norms. But this raises the question, should Christians be like everyone else? To arrive at an answer to this question, we must first establish what it actually means to be a Christian.

Pope Leo the Great († 461), in his Christmas sermons, described being a Christian as follows and connected it with an admonition: "Christian, recognize your dignity! You have become partaker of the divine nature, do not return to the old wretchedness and do not live beneath your dignity." To be a Christian means first to live as new people who have put on Christ as a garment (cf. Gal. 3:27) and are incorporated into the Church. It is about participation in the hierarchical order, whose "Holy Source" is God, through whom the gate to eternal life is opened. The Christian confesses this and follows Christ through faith and the practice of the sacraments.

If we look at the Bible, we can see that exhortations to "be like everyone else" are nothing new and are already present in the Old Testament. However, such behavior was described as a "temptation" (cf. Ezek. 20:32). Those who gave in to it usually fell away from the faith, as evidenced by the example from Exodus of the people's idolatry and dancing around the golden calf (cf. Exod. 32:1–35). The underlying problem is the arrogance of man, who thinks he knows better than God. This ignores the fact that no human being can fathom the Lord's thoughts, not because they are incomprehensible, but because they are so exalted above human thoughts. "My thoughts are not your thoughts, neither are your ways my ways, saith the Lord" (Isa. 55:8). Being a Christian, therefore, presupposes above all the courage to listen to the Divine Word, which alone constitutes communion with God, because He is the Word, and this Word has existed from the beginning (cf. John 1) and awaits man's response.

But because the temptation of the devil is not to have in mind what God wants, but what men want (Mark 8:32), the apostle Paul clearly established those parameters that are valid for all times: "Whoever preaches to you another gospel contrary to what we have preached—let him be accursed" (Gal. 1:8). The apostle is even more explicit when he adds: Is "it then for the approval of men that I am concerned, or is it for God? Do I seek to please men? If I still wanted to please men, I would not be a servant of Christ" (Gal. 1:10).

Here it becomes clear what it means to be Christian. The Christian does not become a Christian by participating in discussions and debates or by advocating for the church to adapt to ever changing social norms. On the contrary, the Christian becomes a Christian by accepting Jesus Christ as the only Savior of mankind and by holding fast to His teaching, which is Jesus Himself. Thus, the Letter to the Romans says: "Do not conform to this world, but be transformed by a new way of thinking, so that you may test and discern what is the will of God, what is good and perfect" (Rom. 12:2).

6

Are all People Children of God: Why is Baptism Needed?

IN TIMES OF PLURALISM, when all differences are treated with suspicion, people like to emphasize that we are all children of God. There might be different religions and creeds, even a plethora of people who define themselves as atheists, but it is said that they are all children of the one God. This statement is used as the basis for a culture of encounter, in order to enable people to live together in tolerance. Additionally, reference is made to the biblical image of man. If man is created in the image of God, then he is also by definition a child of God. But if all people are children of God, what is the need for baptism? The answer to this question requires a clarification of the nature of baptism.

Through the incarnation of Jesus Christ, the Son of God, the order of salvation has fundamentally changed. God became man for us humans and for our salvation, as all Christians testify in the Creed. Salvation—the door to eternal life—does not come by itself but is bound to the acceptance of the truth about Jesus Christ, which is usually made manifest in the sacrament of baptism. But what does baptism mean?

Starting in the Old Testament various texts express the promise that eternal life is given by salvific signs. Above all, the symbolism of water points to this (cf. Gen. 1:2; Exod. 13–16; 1 Pet. 3:20). The promise is fulfilled in Jesus Christ, who, before his ascension, commissions the apostles: "Go therefore and make disciples of all nations, baptizing them in the name of the Father and of the Son and of the Holy Spirit, teaching them to observe all that I have commanded you" (Matt. 28:19–20). This command is not incidental, because baptism is necessary for salvation. As Jesus made clear if "anyone is not born of water and the Spirit, he cannot enter the kingdom of God" (John 3:5).

Baptism is the beginning of participation in the life of God, comparable to a gate through which

Are all People Children of God: Why is Baptism Needed?

the light of divine presence shines into one's life. The baptized person is washed clean of all sin—including original sin—and sealed with an indelible imprint, thus becoming a child of God. Therefore, from the very beginning in the Church, baptism was called rebirth (cf. 1 Pet. 1:3), through which a human child becomes a child of God.

At this point, a fundamental distinction must be made between the order of creation and the order of grace. All human beings are creatures made in the image of God (cf. Gen. 1:27). Accordingly, every human being has an inviolable dignity, which is inscribed in him from conception to natural death and corresponds to the order of creation. The order of grace builds on this but brings with it so much more. Man is not "only" created in the image of God but becomes a "child" of God through baptism. In this, a completely new relationship between God and man comes to exist, for in baptism the baptized person is transformed by sanctifying grace and incorporated into the Church. The "Our Father" is the most beautiful expression of this new relationship between God and the believer. St. Basil attributed a special meaning to the baptismal grace, assuming that from that moment on a Guardian angel is placed at the believer's side as God's protector and shepherd.

In conclusion, all people are creatures of God, but it is only through baptism that a person becomes a child of God. Throughout his life, every baptized person is obliged to respond to this great gift by living a life of faith.

7

Religion Yes, Church No?

AS EARLY AS THE END OF THE 1960s, a development was in the offing that followed the motto: "Religion yes, church no." This expresses the idea that people do need faith, but one free of dogmas and independent of the institutional Church. An institution that imposes dogmatic and moral requirements began to be rejected. According to such a view the church represents manipulation and loss of freedom. Quite a few theologians have jumped on this bandwagon, and although their points were not directed against the Church in general—otherwise they would have made themselves completely superfluous—they raised arguments against the teaching authority of the Church.

The coming to light of scandals and abuse has further reinforced this tendency and is frequently seen as confirmation of the correct nature of this view. The number of people leaving the Church is at a record high in some countries, which makes it clear that the Church is hardly succeeding in communicating why she exists in the first place. This attrition in membership makes the question of whether religion and faith can exist without the Church even more critical. To answer this question, we must clarify "what the Church is."

The Church is an institution, but her nature includes more than a merely human dimension; she is not comparable to a political party nor to an NGO (Non-Governmental Organization). A precise definition of her nature is found in the Dogmatic Constitution of the Church, which states: "The Church is in Christ like a sacrament or as a sign and instrument both of a very closely knit union with God and of the unity of the whole human race" (Vatican II, *Lumen Gentium*, 1). This statement highlights two dimensions of the Church that are inseparable and need further explanation.

The Church consists of a constitutive divine dimension and a human dimension. The head of the Church is Jesus Christ; therefore, it is the image of the invisible God (cf. Col. 1:15–18). All the members of the Church must be conformed to Him (cf. Gal. 4:19). Thus, the inner center of the Church is where the most holiness and the most conformity to God are found. Therefore, the real center of the Church is the Triune God, surrounded by angels and saints.

At the same time, there is a human dimension to the Church. This human dimension is most positively manifest in the witness of the saints. Conversely, the Church's credibility is too often tarnished and damaged by the sins of its fallible members, which disrupts not only harmony with God but also harmony among its members. Whenever this happens, there arises a contradiction to the very task of the Church to be "a sign and instrument" of intimate union with God.

Today, almost everything in the Church seems to revolve only around the human dimension, thereby making the sins and mistakes of some the singular focus. These human failings are frequently used as a pretext for suggesting the need for radical changes in the structure and doctrine of the Church. This overemphasis on the human dimension of the Church obscures both the reality that all human beings are flawed and limited but also the bigger picture of the Church as a divine sign and instrument. This bigger picture is blocked and the understanding of the divine role of the church is absent leaving the church to appear both corruption-laden and superfluous.

To reverse this perilous trend, it is imperative to consider the Church's sacramental dimension, which offers a more complete picture of its nature and purpose. The Church is constituted by God; she has the mission of being the instrument of salvation in order to sanctify the lives of the people through the divine presence. It follows that there is no need for an increase to the human dimension of the Church because it would always be comparatively inferior to its divine dimension. Rather, the emphasis must be placed on the divine, for only then does the reason for the Church's existence become comprehensible. To the extent that an understanding of the Church's divine nature grows among the believers, the Church would equally gain in attractiveness. With this understanding of the role of the Church, it would become clear that there can be no faith and no religion without the Church, whose very task consists in being an instrument for the most intimate union with God.

8

Is the Catholic Church in Possession of the Truth?

TODAY, TRUTH IS OFTEN PERceived as a danger and a limitation. Indeed, if something is true or declared to be true, then—according to a common view—it excludes other beliefs and creates tensions. In a multicultural society, an insistence on the truth is often viewed as offensive, even a threat to social harmony. Not surprising then that we see a certain wariness of a powerful institution like the Catholic Church that makes a bold claim to the truth.

Errors and contradictions are taken as proof that such a claim is no longer tenable today. The Catholic Church, it is said, would do well to be humbler and to renounce its claim to truth. So, the question arises, is the church in possession of the truth?

Let us examine this question in more depth. The renunciation of truth is indeed frequently interpreted as an expression of humility, but in reality, it is the opposite. Those who renounce truth make their own opinions and ideas the "truth." Therefore, the Church's claim to truth not only protects against the arbitrariness of the individual, but it also guarantees fidelity to the origin. Cardinal Joseph Ratzinger made this clear when he said, "To take away from faith the claim to stated and intelligible truth is that false modesty which is the opposite of humility—the non-acceptance of the *condition humaine*, but renunciation of the dignity of being human which makes its sufferings bearable and great" (Joseph Ratzinger, *Wesen und Auftrag der Theologie*, Freiburg 1993, 81).

In reality, truth (cf. John 8:32) liberates man because it provides direction and orientation. The meaning of this statement is revealed in Jesus Christ. He revealed himself as *the* truth (John 14:6), he came to bear witness to the truth, and everyone who is of the truth listens to his voice (cf. John 18:37). The witness to the truth par excellence is love, which gives life (cf. John 15:13) and corresponds to the nature of God (cf. 1 John 4:8),

Is the Catholic Church in Possession of the Truth?

so that the cross and the sacraments, which come from the events of redemption, become the greatest witness to divine truth. In Jesus Christ, the truth of God is fully revealed.

The church is entrusted with this truth of Christ. It has the task of bearing witness to it, "whether convenient or inconvenient" (2 Tim. 4:2). She is the steward of "the manifold gifts of God's grace" (1 Pet. 4:10). The Second Vatican Council aptly expressed this in the Dogmatic Constitution on the Church, recalling that the bishop is "steward of the grace of the supreme priesthood" (Vatican II, *Lumen Gentium*, 26). The pope, the Magisterium and the Church are committed to the service of the truth revealed in Jesus Christ (cf. Vatican II, *Dei Verbum*, 10). In this way, the Church becomes the mouthpiece and witness of that truth which she neither invented nor alters but receives from God himself.

In conclusion, we can answer the question posed earlier. The Church is not in possession of the truth, because whoever possesses something can dispose of it freely. But the Church is "the pillar and foundation of the truth" (1 Tim. 3:15). This truth is not her own, but it is entrusted to her for administration (cf. Luke 16:1–18), and the Lord will require an account of it. Therefore, the Church is obliged to keep the commandments of God and to hold fast to the testimony of Jesus (cf. Rev. 12:17). This can only succeed if she humbly listens to and proclaims the truth, which has revealed itself in Jesus Christ in order to be a co-worker of the truth (cf. 3 John 1:8).

9

May the Church Prescribe a Moral Code?

ODERN MAN LIKES TO invoke the achievements of enlightenment and is reluctant to be dictated to by an institution like the Church. Astonishingly, the opposite is true in the case of decisions by state authorities, particularly during the Covid pandemic, in which the restriction on the most basic civil rights was easily accepted.

Regarding the Church, a contrary trend still prevails, which is also being promoted by many theologians. As early as the 1970s, an attempt was made to establish an "autonomous morality" which—to put it simply—works without authoritative norms. The new source of knowledge is one's own reason, considering one's own understanding of "good" and "evil." Such an attitude still enjoys great approval. Even those who are not versed in theological debates and do not know the basics of faith and morals want to have their say and want to decide for themselves on the question of what is good and evil. Since God is love (cf. 1 John 4:8), then shouldn't it be up to the individual to make personal choices about what is moral and what is not, especially if no one else is seemingly harmed by the choice? Thus, why should it be up to the Church to make regulations, particularly when some of those seem to be opposed to the commandment of love?

In order to answer this question, it is first necessary to clarify the basics. Love is not to be confused with arbitrariness, or with a mere feeling. According to Christian understanding, it is characterized by self-giving. "No one has greater love than this, to lay down one's life for one's friends" (John 15:13). Self-giving, however, implies and requires orientation and direction: it must be clear for *what* one would lay down his life. The earthly life of Jesus Christ provides the model of what it is to witness to the truth, guided by love (cf. Eph. 4:15). He came into this world to offer His life, and through the sacrifice of Himself, He redeemed us. Therefore, there is no true love without sacrifice. However, according to Christian

May the Church Prescribe a Moral Code?

understanding, love only becomes love when it is in accordance with the teaching of the Gospel: "If you love me, you will keep my commandments" (John 14:15); that means remaining in the truth of Christ. In this sense, St. Augustine could say "Love and do what you will" (In Io. Ep. 5,8, PL 35).

Confusingly similar but diametrically opposed to Christianity, on the other hand, is the principle of Satanism as propagated by Aleister Crowley: "There is no law beyond, do what thou wilt!" Autonomy from God and His truth, which is shown in the commandments, corresponds to the basic temptation of the devil to be like God (cf. Gen. 3:5). This danger is always present because our own ideas can easily become opposed to God. Already the prophet Isaiah describes this when he points out that we had all gone astray because everyone went his own way (cf. Isa. 53:6).

In order to be preserved from this, the Lord established the Church as a "pillar and foundation of the truth" (1 Tim. 3:15). It has the task of teaching all people to obey everything that he himself has commanded (Matt. 28:20). This heavy obligation is underscored by the Apostle Paul when he urges his successor to "Preach the word, stand up, whether convenient or inconvenient, convict, rebuke, exhort in all patience and instruction!" (2 Tim. 4:2).

In the past decades, the challenge of witnessing and communicating the liberating effect of truth (cf. John 8:32) has met with little success, particularly regarding the moral teaching of the Church. Truth is not a burden, but a relief, because it gives love its inner direction. Indeed, whoever departs from the truth—which is Christ himself—goes astray and love grows cold. Therefore, the Magisterium, in unbreakable fidelity to revealed truth, has the task and duty of leading the way in the teaching of faith and morals. This service to truth gives love that direction which allows it to develop fully; at the same time, it protects it from the temptation to want to be like God. Pope John Paul II recalled this when he affirmed that the Magisterium, in fidelity to Jesus Christ and in continuity with the tradition of the Church, considers it its duty "to assist man on his journey toward truth and freedom" (John Paul II, *Veritatis Splendor*, 27).

10

The Pope: Infallible?

AT THE FIRST VATICAN COUNcil (1869–1870), papal infallibility was solemnly proclaimed in the dogmatic constitution *Pastor Aeternus*. In reaction, the so-called "Old Catholics" split off from the Church in rejection of this definition as "incompatible with the Gospel." Since then, there have been repeated challenges to papal infallibility. In the early 1970s, the Swiss theologian Hans Küng brought this issue to the attention of the media and the broader public with his book "Infallible. An Inquiry". The discussions about this topic have not abated. So, is the Pope infallible? Or to put it more pointedly: Is he infallible when he speaks out on topics such as migration, ecology or vaccines?

According to the testimony of the New Testament, it is clear that Jesus Christ founded a visible Church with a hierarchical order, in which the Apostle Peter had a special role (cf. Matt. 16:18). To this Church, he promised the assistance of the Holy Spirit to guide it into all truth (cf. John 16:13). And he made the promise that his Church would never stray from truth as a whole (cf. 1 Tim. 3:15). Furthermore, Peter was given the power of binding and loosing (cf. Matt. 16:19) to definitively interpret the faith when necessary and possible. After his conversion—which always consists in turning to God and to the divine commandment—Peter receives the emphatic invitation to strengthen his brothers in the faith (cf. Luke 22:32). Biblically, this is the most urgent task of Peter's ministry and includes the binding interpretation of the faith.

Infallibility corresponds to this supreme teaching authority of the Successor of Peter, making him the guarantor of unity, which is always unity in faith. The First Vatican Council expressed this in 1870. In the process, a realistic picture of the Pope was drawn, which also leaves room for human weaknesses and errors. Therefore, regarding papal infallibility, clear inclusions and limitations have been made. Infallibility belongs to the pope only when he speaks *ex cathedra, that is,* when he decides in the exercise of his pastoral office and by virtue of supreme authority in matters of doctrine of faith and morals.

The Pope: Infallible?

This teaching authority was reaffirmed by the Second Vatican Council (1962–1965), and at the same time it was clarified: The Magisterium is not above the Word of God, "but serves it, teaching nothing but what has been handed down, because it hears with reverence, sacredly preserves and faithfully interprets the Word of God by divine mandate and with the assistance of the Holy Spirit, and because it draws from this one treasure of faith all that it proposes to believe as revealed by God" (Vatican II, *Dei Verbum*, 10).

An infallible doctrinal proclamation by the pope therefore presupposes that: 1) it concerns the doctrine of faith or morals; 2) this doctrine is in no way contrary to Scripture and Tradition; 3) it is solemnly proclaimed (*ex cathedra*) with the highest authority.

On the one hand, it would be a colossal misunderstanding to classify as "infallible" every utterance of the Pope, for example on questions of migration, ecology, vaccination, or a casual remark in an interview, because this would be completely contrary to the nature of the matter. On the other hand, it would be a false humility to deny this God-given authority to the highest authority of the Church. The present situation shows: Wherever this denial occurs, one's own opinion soon takes the place of the authentic

Magisterium, which is then passed off as "infallible." It is a tragedy of the times that those who vigorously reject ecclesiastical infallibility claim it for themselves personally.

11

Is the Church too Fixated on the Sacraments?

PROTESTANT AND SOME Catholic theologians warn against a fixation of Catholics on the sacraments. Such a fixation, they worry, might lead to an individualistic understanding of salvation where the individual would be overly concerned only with his own salvation and forget their commitment to the community of the Church. It is claimed that such a view must be overcome, that it is a relic of a narrowly guided ecclesiology (doctrine of the Church). Is the significance of the sacraments in the Church a relic of medieval piety that must be overcome? Or are there reasons why the Church assigns central importance to the sacraments?

To answer these questions, we must first discuss what a sacrament is. The word is derived *from* the Latin *sacramentum* and is a translation of the Greek word *Mystérion*. It denotes the "means of salvation" through which divine grace is bestowed. Sacraments are not merely symbols that recall, for example, something from the life of Jesus, but they are effective and visible signs of an invisible grace. Accordingly, in each sacrament, an outward sign indicates and communicates an inward grace.

Sacraments are *the* signs of the New Covenant; in them God comes to meet man and man meets God. All seven sacraments are instituted by Christ, he himself works in them, whereby the sacraments of baptism, confirmation and priestly ordination imprint an indelible mark on the person receiving them and can therefore only be validly received once.

All sacraments act *ex opere operato*, that is, by themselves with the action performed through the power of Christ. When they are administered according to their institution by Christ, the sacraments effect grace by virtue of the sacred authority in which the act was performed, even if the minister of the sacrament is living in mortal sin.

All sacraments are sacraments of faith, they become understandable only through this,

Is the Church too Fixated on the Sacraments?

because faith opens the access to the invisible realities which the sacraments signify. In the sacraments, Christ is the actual agent, while the ministers of the sacraments have an instrumental role. They are comparable to an instrument through which the Lord acts. The Church is entrusted with the task of making this treasure (cf. Matt. 13:44) accessible to all people, thus becoming a sign and instrument of the most intimate union with God as well as of the unity of all humanity (cf. Vatican II, *Lumen Gentium*, 1).

This context explains why the sacraments are also called a means of salvation. Through them the body of Christ (the church) is built up and people are sanctified, they are given the gracious relationship with God. Such an understanding has nothing to do with an "individualism of salvation," for the Christian knows that the sacraments are gifts of grace imparted through the Church. Rather, the reception of each sacrament presupposes and strengthens the communion of the faithful with the Church, for no one can administer a sacrament to himself. Whenever the importance and practice of the sacraments diminish in the lives of the faithful, this is by no means an expression of progress, but a loss of God's presence, from which the Church has and retains its raison d'être. For this reason, only when the Church is "fixed" on the sacraments will she be able to fulfill her very mission of making disciples of all peoples (cf. Matt. 28:19).

12

Is There a Difference Between Priests and Lay People?

FOR DECADES, CALLS FOR women to be ordained to the priesthood have been made. Over the years, such demands have led to a new awareness. Some think that the tasks that a priest performs can also be done by any lay person—man or woman—and that a lay person may even be better at performing priestly duties. Following the tradition of Martin Luther, the common priesthood of all believers, which is founded in baptism, is set against the ordained priesthood. This tendency is currently receiving new impetus from the emerging "gender ideology" (cf. Francis, *Amoris laetitia*, 56), which consists in the radical decoupling of the natural difference between men and women. Quite a few people active in ecclesial ministry have been inspired by this ideology and demand the recognition that every baptized person represents Christ and, consequently, can act *in persona Christi*. So, can anyone perform the duties of the priest, is there still a difference between priests and the laity?

To answer this question, we will first define what the priesthood is. The priesthood goes back to Jesus Christ. He came "as high priest of the goods to come" (Heb. 9:11), that is to give salvation. By receiving holy orders, the priest receives an indelible seal, he becomes conformed to Christ and is empowered to act in the name and person of Christ. He "represents" Christ. In this context, however, "representation" is by no means to be understood as a simple proxy, as an ambassador represents his head of government, but it is a real representation in the fullest sense: Jesus Christ is sacramentally present in the priest.

Therefore, the priest is enabled to act in the person of Jesus Christ, that is, Christ acts in and through him. This is particularly evident in the sacraments. For example, at the absolution in confession, the priest says: "I absolve you of your sins. In the name of the Father and of the Son and of the Holy Spirit." Only God can forgive sins (cf. Luke 5:21–25) and it would be more than

Is There a Difference Between Priests and Lay People?

presumptuous for a human being to claim such a thing for himself. God, therefore, acts through the priest. It is the same in the Holy Eucharist when the priest says the words of consecration: "This is my body" and "This is my blood."

It is obvious that this real representation of Christ does *not* become possible by human authority or by virtue of certain qualities, but only when it corresponds to that divine will by whose mandate and authority the priest acts. The Second Vatican Council therefore emphasized that the common priesthood of all the faithful, founded in Baptism, is different in nature from the ordained priesthood (cf. Vatican II, *Lumen Gentium*, 10). However, this can only be understood if the relationship between faith and sacrament is not disturbed: in the priest (external sign) Christ acts (supernatural reality). With this understanding it becomes clear that the priesthood is not about power, but about the service of making Christ and his saving action present.

Pope John Paul II infallibly affirmed that since Jesus Christ came into the world as a man, priestly ordination is reserved only to men who receive divine authority through ordination. The priesthood is first and foremost sacramental and therefore inseparably bound to that testament which Jesus Christ sealed with his blood. Even if the priest differs in essence from the layman, he remains a weak and sinful man. Pope Benedict XVI has described this as follows: "God makes use of a poor man in order to be and act through him for men. This boldness of God, who entrusts himself to people, who trusts people to act and be there for him, even though he knows our weaknesses—this is the truly great thing that is hidden in the word priesthood" (Benedict XVI, Homily of June 11, 2010).

13

Is Confession Outdated?

THE SACRAMENT OF CONFESsion has long been in crisis. Trust in priests has dwindled, not least as a result of scandals. It is said that one cannot confess one's sins to a person who may himself be guilty. Others have turned away from confession because they received counsel that did not correspond to the teachings of the Church and left them confused. Still, others take the view, "Well, I haven't killed anybody," and therefore they do not see the need to go to confession. Among church workers, it is common to find the opinion that the communal celebration of penance, perhaps even with general absolution, can replace confession, since this seems more in keeping with modern trends. So, is confession outdated and a remnant of medieval piety?

The answer to this question requires an understanding of what the Sacrament of Confession is and what it does. Like all seven sacraments, confession was instituted by Jesus Christ and entrusted to the Church for faithful administration: "To those whose sins you remit, they are remitted; to those whose sins you retain, they are retained" (John 20:23). Forgiveness of sins can never be the work of men (cf. Mark 2:6–10) but takes place under the authority of God and through the power of the Holy Spirit. Precisely for this reason it does not take place in an impersonal or general manner, but through that mediation which God has given in Jesus Christ. He is present in the sacrament, speaking through the priest, "I absolve you of your sins."

In the priest, however unworthy and sinful he may be, Christ acts when he administers the sacrament and does what the Church has commanded him to do; this refers above all to the formula of administration and the intention. For the forgiveness of sins, five conditions must be met on the part of the person receiving confession: reflect, repent, confess, atone, amend. Confession is a personal encounter with Jesus Christ in the sacrament. It is preceded by reflection on one's sins and faults, followed by sincere contrition, and a complete confession of all conscious sins;

Is Confession Outdated?

this is followed by penance as part of reparation and a resolution to amend one's life.

Through confession, mortal sins (also called grave sins) that destroy love in the heart of the believer are forgiven. They are a serious violation of God's law and require full awareness and free consent. Not only before receiving sacramental Communion, but also in general, every Catholic is required to examine himself carefully (cf. 1 Cor. 11:27–32) and to ask for forgiveness of sins, because Christ became man for this purpose: to redeem us from our sins.

Even though it is obligatory for every Catholic to receive the Sacrament of Confession at least once a year (cf. can. 989 CIC), confession is not to be understood as a burden but as a liberation. It is comparable to a house cleaning, whereby everything is put back in order: the relationship with God, with neighbor and with oneself. The burden of sin brings people down and makes them fall deeper and deeper. Frequently, people suffering from severe psychological problems are weighed down by sin. It is most important to rediscover the healing effect of the sacrament of confession; it is irreplaceable especially in these times. Therefore, the practice of confession—not participation in general penance services—is considered a criterion for the vitality of a community.

14

Is the Eucharist More than a Meal for All?

IN THE LAND OF THE REFORmation, unease is spreading once again about the "Lord's Table" (the Eucharist) and the fact that some are excluded from receiving communion in the Catholic Church. Inclusion has long been preached, according to which all should be equally invited to participate. The distribution of holy communion across denominations is considered a means of overcoming separation, and it is even seen as a "sign of the times," especially in the context of the massive loss of relevance of institutional churches. Moreover, it is said, that Jesus invites everyone to participate in the meal, and no one should be excluded. For this reason, it should not be up to

Is the Eucharist More than a Meal for All?

the Magisterium of the Church to decide who can participate, but rather it should be up to the responsible Christian to discern for himself according to his own conscience.

These and similar positions are put forward with much emphasis and are frequently based in emotion. To respond to this erroneous view of participation in the Eucharist, it is first necessary to understand what the Eucharist is. Is it merely a meal whose symbolic content wants to point people to the loving presence of God?

God became man to redeem us from our sins. For this purpose, he made the New and Everlasting Covenant in his blood, shed on the cross for the redemption of all people (cf. 2 Cor. 5:14). Under the species of bread and wine, this mystery of faith is made present in the Eucharist. In this way the Scripture is fulfilled: He is the living bread "which came down from heaven. Whoever eats of this bread will live forever" (John 6:51). Already Justin the Martyr (†c. 165), in his Apology and in accordance with tradition, declares that the Eucharist is not an ordinary bread: When the words of prayer of the Eucharist are said over the gifts of bread and wine, that miraculous transformation occurs which makes present the mystery of redemption. Many centuries later, at the time of the Reformation, this belief was massively challenged. Thus, the Council of Trent (1545–1563) felt compelled to define the faith of the Church dogmatically in order to guide the faithful. The concept of transubstantiation, which gives expression to the mystery of faith, lent itself particularly well to this purpose. Through the transformation of the whole substance of the bread into His body and the whole substance of the wine into His blood, Jesus Christ becomes present in the Eucharist.

This transformation of substance makes real the Lord's promise not to leave us orphans (cf. John 14:18). At the same time, it becomes clear that what is at stake is neither a symbolic commemoration nor an ordinary meal, but the real and substantial presence of God in the sacrifice of himself. The priest, acting in the person of Christ, speaks the words of consecration; they are, in a certain sense, words of creation of a new divine reality.

With this understanding, the Apostle Paul gave a clear admonition to the Christians in Corinth. He urged them to make a serious examination of conscience before receiving Holy Communion: "Therefore, whoever eats of the bread and drinks of the cup unworthily is guilty of the body and blood of the Lord. Let each one examine himself; only then let him eat of the bread and drink of the

Is the Eucharist More than a Meal for All?

cup" (1 Cor. 11:29). Receiving the Body and Blood of Christ signifies the most intimate union with God and necessarily implies full communion with Him and His Church. This is called the "state of grace," which is why no one who is conscious of grave sin should receive the Lord's body.

Those who are aware of the greatness of this divine gift necessarily show it by gestures of reverence, such as genuflecting before the Blessed Sacrament on the altar, kneeling in general, and kneeling to receive Communion on the tongue, the proper form of receiving Communion approved by the Church. The clergy make this clear, among other things, by the care and reverence with which they clean the liturgical vessels.

Therefore, the Pauline standard corresponds to the essence of the Eucharist, since the "most holy Eucharist contains the Church's good of salvation in all its fullness" (Vatican II, *Presbyterorum Ordinis*, 5). It is, therefore, not a matter of trivialities, for the Church lives from the Eucharist (cf. John Paul II, *Ecclesia de Eucharistia*, 1); it is the source and summit of the whole of Christian life (Vatican II, *Lumen Gentium*, 11).

15

Can Sundays and Solemnities be Cancelled?

DURING THE "CORONA ERA," most governments took rigorous safety measures, which also restricted the celebration of important high feasts such as Christmas and Easter. The lockdown was a challenge for many people and soon the question arose as to how to deal with it: can a Catholic high feast be celebrated without a church service?

Numerous people in positions of responsibility advised that Church services should be suspended as this would best protect the faithful and their health. Soon enough it was suggested that there could be substitutive celebrations in the home. Others agreed, wanting to signal solidarity with those parts of society that were paralyzed by the measures, by canceling liturgical services. Therefore, one might well ask: is a liturgical solemnity possible without the in-person participation in the Holy Eucharist, or are there alternative ways of celebrating such a feast? To answer this question, it is first necessary to understand the meaning of solemnity. In doing so, we will refer to Christmas as the representative example.

Today, there is often the impression that Christmas is a charming family celebration with sentimental moments, where people meet to comfortably spend time together in harmony. However, such an idea has very little in common with the actual Christmas message. The very fact that Jesus was born in the poverty and the cold of a stable, "because there was no room for them in the inn" (Luke 2:7), speaks a different language. God chose this place, which was unsurpassed in simplicity, so that nothing would distract from the significance of the actual event: the beginning of our redemption.

This is the central Christmas message, as the Church solemnly testifies in the Creed: "For us men and for our salvation He came down from heaven, incarnate through the Holy Spirit from the Virgin Mary." The beginning of our redemption is celebrated and then completed by the sacrifice on the cross. Redemption means redemption from our sins that separate from God. Redemption is accomplished through the sacrifice of the Son of God, who came as mediator between God and men and "gave himself as a ransom for all" (1 Tim. 2:6). Thus, salvation is open to all men of good will (cf. Luke 2:14). Man has only to accept it.

However, then, and now, many reject God. Sacred Scripture describes that all of Jerusalem was greatly troubled by the news of the birth of the Messiah (cf. Matt. 2:3); it even brought about a bloody persecution (cf. Matt 2:16). From this, it follows that the Messiah becomes the "ransom for many" (Mark 10:45), for those who come to the manger and worship Him. Worship thus becomes the sign of God's recognition and acceptance.

This explanation helps to unravel the meaning of Christmas and to answer the question posed at the beginning. Christmas can only be understood by those who, like the Magi from the East, bow their knees in adoration before the greatness of God. The Fathers of the Church already interpreted the manger allegorically as an altar, because the Lord became man in order to redeem us, and redemption becomes present in the Eucharist. That is why the Holy Mass belongs inseparably to Christmas and cannot be replaced by anything or anyone, just as Jesus Christ cannot be replaced, without him there is no Christmas.

For faithful Christians, the most important objective in life is not health, but eternal life. In times of crises, wars, and epidemics, the Church has continually multiplied its prayers and renewed her trust in God. When Christmas, Easter, or even "just" the ordinary Sunday Mass are canceled, the encounter with the One who alone has "words of eternal life" (John 6:68) is missing. The early Christians in Carthage (around the year 300), for example, preferred to die than to forgo Sunday Mass; they could not live without Sunday. They were aware that the Church—and thus they themselves—live from the Eucharist.

16

Is Mary a Role Model for Self-Determination and Women's Rights?

IN RECENT YEARS, DEMANDS have arisen to change the structure of a male-dominated Church. Several initiatives and actions have been undertaken to push for the ordination of women. The name "Mary" has often been brought up in support of this call for the ordination of women. Mary—in the 2.0 version—is supposed to embody a woman who did not allow herself to be silenced, who stood up for her rights and—if necessary—fought for them. In this context, certain representatives even go so far as to ascribe to Mary attributes such as "co-founder of the church." The question

Is Mary a Role Model for Self-Determination

therefore arises as to who Mary is and what does she stand for? An answer to these questions requires first a recollection of the basic truths about Mary without which no understanding is possible.

Mary, the Mother of God, is inseparably connected with the mystery of salvation revealed in Jesus Christ. As true God and true man, he was born of the Virgin Mary (cf. *Credo*). Already in this passage it becomes clear that Mary—like no other creature—is included in the mystery of God. Mary receives everything from God, she is the one who receives everything and thus becomes the archetype of the Church (cf. Vatican II, *Lumen Gentium*, 53). In Sacred Scripture, therefore, she is described with the attribute "full of grace" (Luke 1:28). Mary expresses her unconditional consent to the divine plan of salvation with the words: "I am the handmaid of the Lord; let it be done to me according to your word" (Luke 1:38).

By grace and her free consent, Mary becomes the God-bearer, as dogmatically defined by the Council of Ephesus (431 AD). This truth of faith is to be understood above all Christologically, since it recalls the divine and human nature of Jesus Christ. Mary as a creature conceives the God-Man, whereby Mary uniquely enters into the mystery of the Triune God. She is the daughter of the Father, the bride of the Holy Spirit, and the mother of the Son, in view of His human nature.

A correct understanding of Mary is revealed through faith, which presupposes the acceptance of God's revelation. It is necessary to avoid a twofold narrowness: a) the denial of the true divinity of Christ, which leads to the denial of the title "God-bearer"; b) the denial of the true humanity of Christ, which leads to the denial of the true motherhood of Mary.

The current debates make it clear that the belief in the true deity of Christ, from whom alone salvation and redemption are given, is in danger of being lost. In antiquity, the patriarch of Constantinople, Nestorius (†c. 453), had advocated such a false doctrine, although his subtle argumentation can by no means be compared with the clumsy objections of the present time.

When salvation through faith is no longer recognized and accepted as a gift of God, in the way God has wrought it, then demands and appeals for rights and equality take its place. But a closer look shows how absurd this is, because since when is the creature equal to the Creator?

Mary, the Mother of God, calls herself "handmaid" and praises her "lowliness" (Luke 1:48), because she knows that the dignity of the Christian is to be raised by God, through His grace.

Thus, Mary is the highest and holiest creature, surpassing in holiness even the apostles, all the angels and the saints. This becomes possible only through the humble acceptance of Redemption according to the Divine Plan. Accordingly, the demands made under the title "Mary 2.0" have nothing, but really nothing at all in common with Mary, the Mother of God.

17

Angels and Saints: More than an Edifying Tale?

THE BELIEF IN ANGELS enjoys a boom today, but they are largely appropriated by esoteric circles. "Angel amulets," "Angel cards," "Archangels" are increasingly very common. Many Christians, however, have a broken relationship with angels, as well as with the saints. This broken relationship is usually the result of rationalism and the theology influenced by it. As a result, the relation to what is called "supernatural," which includes angels and saints, has been neglected and even challenged. Although angels are mentioned in Sacred Scripture, such as the archangels Michael, Gabriel, and Raphael, or saints, such as Elijah, Moses, and John the Baptist, they

Angels and Saints: More than an Edifying Tale?

nevertheless seem to have little role in the daily life of the faithful. This is particularly evident in the celebration of the Holy Eucharist, which is the most excellent place to encounter this supernatural reality. Most faithful are no longer aware of this supernatural dimension and therefore it hardly touches their lives. Therefore, these questions emerge: Is the reference to angels and saints more than a pious fairy tale? What is their importance in the lives of believers?

An answer to these questions becomes possible if we first clarify what angels and saints are. Angels are mentioned in both the Old and New Testaments. In the New Testament they appear at all the important events of salvation, such as the birth (cf. Luke 1:26–37), and resurrection (cf. Luke 24:23) of the Lord. They are purely spiritual beings who surpass all visible creatures except Mary in perfection; they are messengers of God. Nine "choirs" of angels can be distinguished, with each "choir" characterizing a particular attribute of the angels. In contrast to demons, the fallen angels, Angels serve God unceasingly. However, they also have important tasks on earth. Not only are they present at every Holy Mass, as witnessed not least by *the* song of the angels ("Holy, holy, holy"), but every believer has

63

a guardian angel at his or her side throughout life (cf. Catechism of the Catholic Church, 336).

It is different with the saints: they were people who lived on earth and came to the beatific vision of God only after death. Therefore, the day of their death is considered their "birthday" into eternal life and is celebrated in the liturgy. In order to enter into the contemplation of the thrice-holy God, Saints first had to become free from every stain of sin through purification. Thus, they participate in communion with the Holy One, from which their name "saints" is derived. Since they live in the presence of God, they are mediators and can intercede for us with their intercession. After relevant examination, the Church recognizes their heroic degree of virtue during life through canonization. Like the angels, there are degrees of sanctity corresponding to their degree of perfection.

Angels and saints make up the majority of those who belong to the Church and constitute the pulsating center of the Church. From there it becomes also understandable why there can be no majority votes in the Church. Rather, angels and saints remind us that the goal of the Christian life is ordered towards the holy origin ("hierarchy"), namely the communion with God. On the way there, angels and saints are not only our role models, but they also want to help people on earth. Through their intercession, great graces can be obtained, as countless answers to prayer and miracles testify. Therefore, it is part of the very tradition of faith to venerate them and to invoke them constantly in prayer.

18

Heaven for all — or, What Comes After Death?

THE MOST FUNDAMENTAL OF all questions is ignored by most people today: what happens after death? Even many Christians are no longer able to answer this question. Therefore, Far Eastern influences are spreading even among some Catholics. Ideas such as transmigration or reincarnation become attractive. Conversely, if a priest dares to speak about hell during a sermon it is generally ill-received. Thus, most of them speak exclusively of heaven, in keeping with a German Carnival Hymn that emphatically assures the listener that all will go to heaven.

This is not new. Already in the early church, the doctrine of *apokatastasis* (restoration) was promulgated, according to which at the end of time God reconciles all people with Himself and gives them heaven, in accordance with God's nature, which is love (cf. 1 John 4:8). Some theologians even postulate that there will be an "empty hell."

So, what comes after death and do all people really go to heaven? An answer to this question can be found neither in the subjective experience of individuals nor in Far Eastern insights, but only in the revelation of God through the incarnation of Jesus Christ. He came into the world, as the *Creed* testifies, for us human beings and for our salvation. "Salvation" in the full sense of the word only happens if death, which entered into the world through sin, is overcome (cf. Rom. 5:12). Jesus Christ is therefore rightly called "Savior," because through his death he overcame death (cf. Rom. 5:19) by "giving himself as a ransom for all" (1 Tim. 2:6).

People have always been aware that ultimately only God is able to grant salvation because it transcends any human power; this granting has definitively happened in Jesus Christ. Theology calls this an "objective salvation," which is valid for all people at all times. It is explicitly God's will for "everyone to be saved and to come to knowledge of the truth" (1 Tim. 2:4).

However, this objective salvation is not automatic, it is not self-realizing. The salvation obtained through Jesus Christ once and for all must be accompanied by a personal acceptance of Christ. This "subjective salvation" respects the personal freedom of the individual. Therefore, the Last Supper account says, "This is my blood of the covenant, which will be shed on behalf of many for the forgiveness of sins." (Matt. 26:28). This passage emphasizes that the covenant becomes effective for the individual when he is ready to accept the redemption brought by Christ and thus accept Jesus Christ himself. The new and eternal covenant—which by its nature must be eternal—presupposes a personal decision through which salvation becomes fruitful in one's own life.

In Jesus Christ, God reveals his plan of salvation for the world and belief in Him or lack thereof leads to clear separation. He is the cornerstone, "'whoever believes in it shall not be put to shame.' Therefore, its value is for you who have faith, but for those without faith: 'The stone which the builders rejected has become the cornerstone,' and 'A stone that will make people stumble, and a rock that will make them fall'" (1 Pet. 2:6–8). According to this logic, immediately after death follows the particular judgment, as defined in an infallible way by the Church (cf. Pope Benedict XII, *Benedictus Deus*). Whoever has accepted Jesus Christ in his lifetime, enters immediately into the Kingdom of Heaven after death, if there is no further need for purification. However, those who still need it, go through a purification process in what is known as purgatory, in order to become ready to enter the beatific vision of God. Whoever, on the other hand, has decided against God through an unrepented mortal sin, will suffer eternal damnation.

The Gospel is rightly understood as "good news" because it shows a concrete way which — if followed — leads to eternal life. The admonition applies: "Go through the narrow gate! For wide is the gate and broad is the way that leads to destruction, and there are many who go through it. How narrow is the gate and how strait the way that leads to life, and there are few who find it" (Matt. 7:13–14).

AFTERWORD

ONLY A LIMITED SELECTION OF TOPics could be considered in this booklet. They are intended to provide guidance to those people who are of goodwill (cf. Luke 2:14), and who with an earnestness of heart seek to find the way to the Lord but struggle against the headwinds of contradictory opinions. Then as well as today, Jesus' urgent admonition comes true: "Many false prophets will arise and deceive many; and because of the increase of evildoing, the love of many will grow cold" (Matt. 24:11–12).

Faith is not a complicated structure of theories, but simple and thus fundamentally accessible to every human being. This simplicity has been lost in many areas of theology. Theologians often hide behind eloquent statements that are difficult to understand philosophically and frequently use them as a pretext to deviate from the truth of the gospel. Referring to an alleged "development of doctrine" or "latest findings" also from the field of social sciences, they construct contradictions which they pass off as "further development". This leads to the absurd situation in which parts of theology have become incapable of giving answers to the simplest questions of faith, such as about the existence of hell, the devil or certain commandments in the field of moral theology whose biblical foundation is beyond any doubt.

In contrast, the Gospel says: "Let your 'Yes' mean 'Yes,' and your 'No' mean 'No.' Anything more is from the evil one" (Matt. 5:37). Pope Benedict XVI, one of the greatest intellectuals and thinkers on the Chair of Peter, has repeatedly emphasized: "Faith is simple. We believe in God, who is the Beginning and End of human life. We believe in a God who enters into a relationship with us human beings, who is our origin and our future" (Benedict XVI, Homily, 12 September 2006).

Simplicity in faith is a prerequisite for its acceptance: "Unless you repent and become like children, you will not enter the kingdom of heaven" (Matt. 18:3). In the Gospel, this simplicity is described as childlike faith, which is by no means to be confused with childish faith. Rather, it is the fruit of that filiation to God which is graciously bestowed through baptism. It is an expression of deep trust in the Lord, who *is* real and gives life a new and definite direction. This is reflected in the "Our Father" as well as in the prayer that the Lord addresses to the Father: "I praise you, Father, Lord of heaven and earth, because you have hidden these things from the wise and prudent and revealed them to babes" (Matt. 11:25).

This reveals the inner logic of faith. It is based on the word of God and this "word is truth" (John 17:17). It is true at any time and in any culture, because "the word of God is living and effective, sharper than any two-edged sword […]. No creature is concealed from him, but everything is naked and exposed to the eyes of him to whom we must render an account" (Heb. 4:12–13).

As important as the knowledge of truth is, it becomes credible only in love. The best arguments will be of little use if faith is not lived and witnessed daily. In order to make this possible, guidance and orientation are needed, to which this booklet would like to make a small contribution.